FLORIDA HOSPITAL *Healthcare & Leadership* MONOGRAPH SERIES

MONOGRAPH VOLUME IV

Making History Together

HOW TO CREATE INNOVATIVE STRATEGIC ALLIANCES TO FUEL THE GROWTH OF YOUR COMPANY

KEITH LOWE, JD, MBA

FLORIDA
HOSPITAL

Since 1908

FLORIDA HOSPITAL
HEALTHCARE
& LEADERSHIP
MONOGRAPH SERIES

MAKING HISTORY TOGETHER
Copyright © 2009 Keith Lowe
Monograph Volume 4
Published by Florida Hospital
683 Winyah Drive, Orlando, Florida 32803

TO EXTEND *the* HEATH *and* HEALING MINISTRY *of* CHRIST

GENERAL EDITOR	Todd Chobotar
WRITER	Lisa Levine
COPY EDITOR	Ken Walker
EXTERNAL PEER REVIEW	Jonathan Hughes
	Terry Newmyer, MBA
INTERNAL PEER REVIEW	Ted Hamilton, MD, MBA
	Diana Boyce
PROMOTION	Stephanie Rick
PROJECT COORDINATION	Lillian Boyd
PHOTOGRAPHY	Spencer Freeman
DESIGN	The Herman Lewis Design Sydicate

Library of Congress Cataloging-in-Publication Data
Lowe, Keith
Making History Together / by Keith Lowe
p. cm.
1. Strategic Alliances (Business). 2. Joint Ventures.
3. Partnership. I. Title II. Florida Hospital
ISBN-13: 978-0-9820409-6-6

Printed in the United States of America
FP 10 9 8 7 6 5 4 3 2 1

For volume discounts please contact special sales at:
HealthProducts@FLHosp.org | 407-303-1929

For more resources on Whole Person Health please visit:
FloridaHospitalPublishing.com

CONTENTS

EDITOR'S INTRODUCTION

"**P**OWERFUL." "INSPIRING." "PARADIGM-SHATTERING." These are terms I've heard used to describe what may be the most transformative question in the field of strategic alliances. The question? *How do we make history together?*

It's so powerful because the question captures the imagination and pushes partners to think bigger and broader. It causes companies and their executives to look beyond short-term sales bumps and feel-good PR campaigns to focus instead on creating new products, services, and solutions that can transform entire industries.

When Keith Lowe and I began discussing ideas for this monograph I was intrigued. Keith's message seemed simple enough. To fuel the growth of your company create strategic alliances focused on innovation—not just selling products or services to each other more cheaply. As simple as the concept may sound, creating and maintaining such relationships can be difficult at best, disastrous at worst. Keith knows this territory well. For years he has led the Strategic Venture Group at Florida Hospital.

I'm not aware of another hospital in America that conducts strategic alliances quite like Florida Hospital in either quantity or quality. That's not to say Florida Hospital has a perfect model or a flawless track record. Keith would be the first to tell you we have made our fair share of mistakes. But that's one of the real values of this monograph. Here Keith lays out hard-won wisdom gained over years of experience and dozens of alliance relationships.

That brings us back to the question: *How do we make history together?* Answer: By dreaming big dreams your company can't accomplish alone, but can accomplish with innovation-infused strategic alliances. In these pages Keith provides a roadmap for creating and sustaining effective alliances with innovation at the core. It's an exhilarating journey you won't want to miss.

Todd Chobotar, General Editor

FOREWORD

INNOVATION IS KEY TO SOLVING THE MYRIAD challenges to America's broken healthcare system. In the coming years, the most successful healthcare companies will continually seek to change the way doctors and hospitals work in order to provide the highest-quality patient care, and in the most accessible and affordable manner.

So it is enlightening to read Keith Lowe's account of Florida Hospital's use of strategic alliances as a catalyst for innovation—both for its insight into the philosophical and structural underpinnings of the hospital's alliance strategy, and for its accounts of its successful alliances with other companies.

Lowe begins with the story of Florida Hospital's first forays into strategic alliances as it worked to design and build an innovative new hospital in Celebration, Florida. At the time (in the early 1990s), strategic alliances were rare in the healthcare industry, so their use at Celebration Health was in itself an innovation. He then provides a useful definition of the term "strategic alliance," with further explanation of the conditions under which these alliances thrive.

As Lowe makes clear, all strategic alliances are not alike. Using Florida Hospital's experiences and requirements as a compass, Lowe shows the various types of relationships companies can form—including their purposes and goals. He also provides illustrative examples of Florida Hospital's experiences with each type of alliance.

Among the more insightful features of this monograph is its pairing of corporate alliance strategy with the mandate for innovation. As Lowe points out, innovation is essential for healthcare companies seeking to meet the present-day and future challenges of their industry. Strategic alliances provide a powerful tool for such innovation. Lowe notes that, in addition to providing the potential for technological and medical breakthroughs, some of the greatest potential for healthcare innovation lies in nontraditional areas. Among them are business models, core processes, and customer experience.

This monograph is essential reading for anyone seeking a succinct primer on strategic alliances. And, for those in the healthcare industry who are using or exploring the use of strategic alliances as a tool for innovation. While the journey of alliance and innovation isn't easy, it is well worth taking, as Florida Hospital's results demonstrate.

I hope this monograph is a great success. It's a message the worlds of business and healthcare need to hear.

Jason Hwang, M.D., M.B.A.

Co-Founder & Executive Director of Healthcare

Innosight Institute, Inc.

Co-Author of *The Innovator's Prescription*

THE DREAM: WALT DISNEY COMPANY AND CELEBRATION HEALTH

FLORIDA HOSPITAL'S EARLIEST EXPLORATION of crafting deeper relationships with other companies—our first strategic alliances—began with a dream.

The year was 1993 and the venture was Florida Hospital's mission to design and build a "hospital of the future" in Celebration, Florida—a town developed by the Walt Disney Company just outside Walt Disney World. The Town of Celebration is the Disney Company's effort to fulfill Walt's original vision for Epcot—the Experimental Prototype City of Tomorrow. Walt had imagined a city where people could live, work, and play, with state-of-the-art technology supporting infrastructure such as education and healthcare. The Epcot at Disney World had been built as a theme park; now Celebration was going be the municipal Epcot that Walt had dreamed of. And Disney chose Florida Hospital to build a hospital and healthcare center in Celebration that would showcase the latest medical trends and technology, with the goal of making the town the healthiest community in the world.

So Florida Hospital's Celebration Health project leaders met with leaders from every hospital department to ask this question: If you could build your department from scratch and money were no object, what would be the very best way to deliver the services you offer? From those discussions, the project leaders began to craft a design for a hospital that would use the most forward-thinking healthcare principles and up-to-the-moment technology to achieve the best possible outcomes for patients.

But such unlimited ambition is rarely accompanied by unlimited resources. Learning about and acquiring the latest medical equipment at every level, from beds to surgical equipment to imaging equipment, is a vastly expensive proposition. So early in the process, the project leaders realized they would need to fashion a new type of business arrangement with suppliers to realize their vision of a futuristic hospital. Achieving this goal meant Florida Hospital needed to leverage the resources of others as well as its own. It needed something more than traditional vendor relationships. Key suppliers needed to be engaged as allies so that Florida Hospital could benefit from their most creative thinking and passionate commitment to shared goals.

At the time, the use of strategic alliances was on the rise, especially among technology companies. However, they were not common in healthcare. Still, Celebration Health project leaders were inspired by Disney's use of strategic alliances as a core strategy for securing revenue, especially evident in the Epcot theme park's Future World pavilions, where leaders in many industries showcase the next wave in technology. Florida Hospital decided to approach key suppliers—who were medical industry leaders—in hopes those companies would share in their vision for a hospital that showcased the next wave of innovation in medicine.

> Such a strategic venture would have benefits for Florida Hospital Celebration Health and its suppliers, which went beyond those found in the usual relationship of buyer and seller. When alliance companies installed their next generation of solutions, the hospital would become their real-world demonstration site. Celebration Health's patients and staff would benefit from access to the latest technology, which would be continually replaced with the next generation of technology as research and development moved forward.

Its allies would get the benefit of feedback from Celebration staff about how well its products functioned in a hospital setting, enhancing their R&D efforts. The alliance companies' prospective buyers could visit Celebration Health to see the equipment being used and question the staff about it. Such an alliance would indeed be strategic for all players in that it would accomplish their goals.

Many of Florida Hospital's existing suppliers welcomed the opportunity to gain a living laboratory in which to introduce their newest developments. Florida Hospital built a consortium of allies, some of which were already established allies of Disney. They brought their best ideas to help design and equip the hospital of the future in Celebration and share in the new vision of how health and wellness would be delivered.

When Florida Hospital Celebration Health opened in 1997, it quickly became one of the most visited hospitals in the country. Medical groups toured the facility to see state-of-the-art medicine in practice. In addition to having the latest technology, equipment, and services, the hospital was designed from a patient-centered viewpoint that changed both the delivery of services and the very nature of the patient experience.

One of the hospital's most striking features is that it doesn't *feel* like a hospital; it looks and feels more like a resort. And it isn't *just* a hospital. With its twin missions to heal and to promote health, it has facilities to treat the mind, body, and spirit, and to maintain the health of the mind, body, and spirit. Clustered near the open and airy entrance lobby and along the main corridor, called the "Avenue of Health," are a large, active fitness center and day spa and a café that serves fresh, delicious dishes instead of bland "hospital food."

The overall design makes extensive use of natural light and gardens to promote well-being. In the treatment areas and throughout the back corridors, called the "Street of Healing," most of the more intimidating trappings of a hospital are kept away from the view of patients and their families. Patients move through a welcoming "onstage" corridor that resembles a hotel corridor, while staff and equipment traverse the "backstage" areas. Sound and lighting are carefully managed so that a serene atmosphere prevails. And, of course, both the practice of medicine and the technology that supports it are continually evaluated and updated to incorporate the most recent advances in healthcare.

Such industry-leading innovation would have been impossible—or at least highly unlikely to succeed—if Florida Hospital had attempted to take on the entire burden of designing and building Celebration Health.   However, it invited top players in the healthcare industry to join in a network that would participate in the risks and rewards in order to realize a shared core vision. By assembling a consortium of strategic alliances, the "hospital of the future" came to fruition in the present. And by all measures of patient satisfaction and of financial return, this "pie-in-the-sky" project is a model for success.

That's the power of strategic alliances.

WHAT IS A STRATEGIC ALLIANCE?

DEFINITIONS ARE IMPORTANT—EVEN ESSENTIAL. Failure to establish a common vocabulary in a relationship can lead to chaos. For example, family relationships don't work as well as they should if there is not an agreed-upon definition of what it means to be a part of the family. And employment relationships function more smoothly if there is a clear understanding of what "work" is. Think about how important it has become over the past thirty years in business to develop statements of mission, vision, and values. All of these are intended to define the organization. The definition of "strategic alliance" is important and arguably the most basic and foundational element of beneficial alliances. This monograph presents our definition of what we at Florida Hospital mean by "strategic alliance." Our goal here is to provide a foundational understanding of strategic alliances that can be applied in healthcare and most any other industry.

The strategic alliance program at Florida Hospital has expanded significantly since the early days of Celebration Health. Through the years, it has included many Fortune 500 companies (see the full list in Appendix), and the most productive relationships continue to generate new opportunities and create value.

As the number of our strategic relationships increased, Florida Hospital created a dedicated alliance resource called the Strategic Venture Group to provide internal leadership and support for its strategic alliances. I currently serve as its executive director. As an attorney new to alliance work several years ago, I remember being frustrated by the lack of a clear technical, legal definition for "alliance." Many in our organization and others seemed to proceed as though there were an agreed-upon definition. But I was having trouble wrapping my head around it. Others were using the term "partnership" as a synonym for alliance, and I was clear that what was being described as a "partnership" was not what the State of Florida case law and statutes had established. Fact is, there is no common law definition of *alliance,* and most statutes (state and federal) are silent on the topic.   It is not one of the recognized legal "entities" studied in law schools today. Furthermore, the technical definition of "partnership" carries with it certain legal obligations and connotations that do not necessarily pertain to the intent of a strategic alliance. The irony is that many alliance documents take great care to specify that the relationship *is not* a partnership.

It has been my experience that most attorneys drafting these documents don't get too hung up on the title of the "alliance agreement" because it really is an exercise in contract drafting, which requires the intent to be reflected in solid definitions set out in the contract.

While strategic alliances may share elements with recognized legal partnership entities, such as some level of mutual commitment and contribution of resources, you'll find at least four key differences:

1. **Responsibility.** Companies in a strategic alliance generally are not responsible for the acts of the other member or members of the alliance.

2. **Duration.** The relationship agreed upon in a strategic alliance is often of shorter duration (as compared to a general partnership).

3. **Risk/Reward.** Depending on the goals and structure of the alliance, the allies may not necessarily share profits or losses (though alliances generally do include some form of risk and reward sharing).

4. **Flexibility.** By design, the agreement reflecting the intent of the allies may not be all-inclusive. Alliances are dynamic relationships that need to be flexible as the relationship and new opportunities develop over time.

So what is a strategic alliance? Here is our working definition at Florida Hospital:

> A strategic alliance is a long-term, collaborative relationship between two or more entities that agree to share complementary resources and capabilities for the purpose of creating strategic value for each organization.

Let's look more closely at the main components of that definition.

• *Long-term.* At Florida Hospital, the strategic alliances we form with other companies generally have an initial term of five years. Why? We feel that a joint project that could be completed in less than five years may not be significant enough in scope or achievement to warrant entering into the alliance. Strategic alliances require significant investments and involve risks and rewards that impact both parties and that will, in most cases, take at least five years to achieve. In addition, a five-year commitment allows the relationship to work through short-term challenges for the potential of the longer term return on investment (ROI). In most cases, a term of five years gives strategic projects enough time to be accomplished and evaluated. After that time, both parties should have enough information to decide whether the collaborative relationship has succeeded in providing value for both parties. If the answer is yes, then the relationship is renewed and is usually broader than the initial relationship, encompassing multiple initiatives.

- *Collaborative.* A strong, strategic alliance is formed when both parties recognize that together they can do something that neither can accomplish as well on its own. Collaboration is not simply cooperation; collaboration requires that the allies make and achieve joint commitments and establish shared goals. It requires a commitment of each party to the success of the other rather than a unilateral definition of success. Learning to be collaborative is key to achieving real value in the alliance—otherwise it's an arm's-length transaction. It is best not to confuse the two. If one party enters into the alliance for purposes of truly creating long-term, strategic value through collaboration and the other cloaks its real intent for short-term economic wins, it makes for a frustrating (and in most cases, short-term) relationship.

- *Strategic value.* We intentionally define a strategic alliance as a relationship that advances the strategies of both companies. The relationship's strategic value can and probably will be different for each member of an alliance. We are not saying that the strategies need to be the same. However, the potential to create strategic value for all allies must be present in order to make a strategic alliance sustainable and worth the effort.

- *For each organization.* This is the mutual benefit component of the definition that presumes a win–win relationship. Obviously, the "strategic value" being sought here is not the benefit exchanged in an arms-length transaction for the sale of products or services to a customer.

In order to move to mutual creation of strategic value, both parties need to move past the traditional "buy/sell" thinking into transparent strategy discussions. In the context of our alliances at Florida Hospital, the corporate strategy for a seller should not be limited to increasing its market share at Florida Hospital. The real question for a seller moving to ally should be: "How can we leverage the resources at Florida Hospital to reach the world with our mission?"

Although not alluded to in the definition, **innovation** is at the center of our alliance strategy at Florida Hospital. We recognize that to achieve our mission, innovation is essential, and that to achieve greater levels of innovation will require inputs from trusted allies. While it is rather common in the healthcare industry for a hospital to purchase the latest medical device and call it "innovation," we would suggest it is difficult to *purchase* strategically valuable and sustainable innovation.

Innovation that changes companies and industries requires a unique relationship that engages the passion and imagination of allies with a shared vision for the future and the shared commitment to make it reality. These are not the elements typically found in the transactional relationship with suppliers; therefore, we need trusted allies to truly innovate. We'll look at the fundamental value of innovation in greater depth in the section titled "Why Is Innovation at the Core?"

STRATEGIC ALLIANCES AND "BLUE OCEAN STRATEGY"

TO BETTER DESCRIBE OUR OBJECTIVES in alliance work and distinguish from traditional trading relationships, we have found it helpful to refer to "Blue Ocean Strategy," a concept introduced in a 2005 book by W. Chan Kim and Renée Mauborgne.[1] The goal of Blue Ocean Strategy is not to outperform the competition in the shark-infested red ocean, but rather to move to the uncontested blue ocean market space where competition is irrelevant. Blue Ocean Strategy is really about finding and creating new markets to better meet the needs of customers.

As an apt example, the book's authors point to Cirque du Soleil vs. Ringling Bros. and Barnum & Bailey Circus. In 1984, the circus was a dying industry with limited growth possibilities, decreasing attendance, and revenues dropping like a rock. Enter Cirque du Soleil. While other circus companies were trying (and mostly failing) to imitate Ringling Bros., fighting for a share of the same audiences, Cirque reimagined the entire concept of the circus. Cirque did not draw from the existing market that catered to children, but rather created a new market targeted to adults and corporate customers willing to pay a nice multiple of the going ticket price. Since 1984, Cirque has thrilled audiences (over 400 million people) in more than ninety cities around the world. And in less than twenty years, Cirque du Soleil earned a level of revenue that took Ringling Bros. more than 100 years to achieve.

So our question is, how do we expand the transactional relationship with companies from the typical "red ocean," where products and services become commodities, into "blue ocean"—new markets—to better achieve our mission? For example, how do we at Florida Hospital expand the current definition of "continuum of care" to include offerings that will help people with chronic disease manage their health from home ("blue ocean," i.e., Cirque) rather than having to return to the hospital ("red ocean," i.e., Ringling Bros.)? Or, how can we transform the patient experience at the hospital such that it would put the patient at ease, lower the need for sedation, and accelerate the healing process? We need alliances to help us accomplish this type of Blue Ocean thinking. While products in the vendor catalogue may have impact, Florida Hospital has teams of people to sort through the best options available in the market today.

What we are really looking for in the alliance program are allies to innovate solutions that don't currently exist.

The graphic below illustrates the transition we seek to achieve with our suppliers.

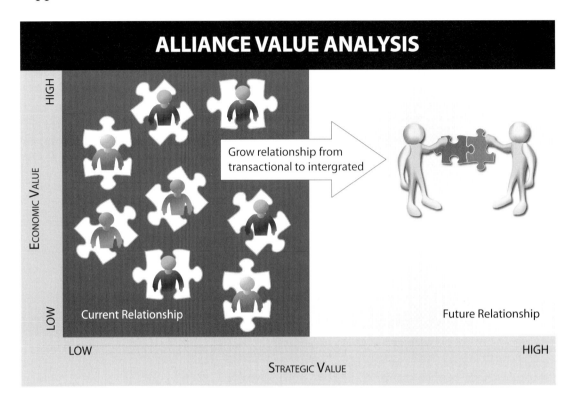

MANY GOALS CAN BE ACCOMPLISHED WITHOUT A STRATEGIC ALLIANCE

NOT EVERY BUSINESS RELATIONSHIP NEEDS to come to the level of a strategic alliance. In fact, we have chosen to limit the number of these relationships at Florida Hospital because of the significant investment and attention required to increase success rates. If there is a more direct means for us or a potential alliance company to accomplish our respective goals, we believe these options should be fully explored before entering into an alliance.

In the day-to-day activity of a hospital, a **transactional** relationship is an acceptable means to accomplish both companies' goals. In this typical vendor–purchaser relationship, the focus is on commodities in the supply chain. The primary drivers for the hospital are cost and quality and the primary drivers for the vendor are increased sales and/or margins. While these relationships are critical to our future success, a strategic alliance is most likely not required or helpful to accomplish both companies' goals.

Sometimes a company can achieve a specific goal on its own by **growing organically**, using or refining the competencies and resources it has already developed. For example, several years ago, Florida Hospital determined it would be best to build its own IT solution that could meet the unique needs of a large healthcare provider. There was not a vendor in the market with a solution that would meet the demands, so we rallied the internal talent and built it internally. Many elements of that solution still exist today. The decision was expensive in the short run but has proved critical to being considered a leader in healthcare IT today.

Or, if it has the means (i.e., access to capital), a company can accomplish some goals by acquiring assets or competencies through a **merger-and-acquisition strategy**, which will not require the input or resources of third parties in the alliance context. Generally there is a premium to be paid for this type of access to new assets and markets, but buying the growth of another company can be an effective strategy for many companies with an abundance of cash.

When a company has growth goals it can meet through strategic procurement, through using its own internal capabilities, or through buying or merging with another company that has those capabilities, a strategic alliance may not be the best vehicle to meet those goals. But there are some circumstances in which a strategic alliance can be a very powerful tool for achieving the goals of all the parties involved, and we'll look at those circumstances next.

WHY DO WE NEED STRATEGIC ALLIANCES?

COOPERATION BETWEEN TWO OR MORE COMPANIES in the form of a strategic alliance can improve each company's performance and fulfill each company's mission in ways those companies would be hard-pressed to accomplish on their own. In an ideal alliance, the parties each bring to the table specialized skills or resources to which the other parties do not have ready access. Those combined skills and resources are used in an endeavor to create unique value for the allies and customers they exist to serve.

In some cases, the aim of this strategic cooperation is **to fuel the growth engine** of one or both parties. At Florida Hospital, we have helped our alliance companies accelerate products to market faster by providing a unique platform as one of the largest hospitals in the United States. Our standing as a large, community-based healthcare system with multiple campuses, ranging from 50 to more than 1,000 beds, provides a perfect product and service "test track" for alliance companies to demonstrate outcomes in both small and large systems. And by working with our allies to accelerate products to market, Florida Hospital cements its reputation as an industry leader and early adopter of technology, fast-tracking solutions for our community.

Other times, an alliance is a useful tool with which **to prepare for and meet future challenges** in the industries in which the companies compete. For example, Florida Hospital is the largest Medicare provider in the United States as of this writing, and our patient demographics are a snapshot of what the rest of the country will look like in the future. As such, there may be no better place in the world to efficiently collaborate to rapidly achieve a competitive advantage, while helping Florida Hospital realize its vision to become a "global pacesetter delivering preeminent healthcare."

But perhaps the most exciting function of strategic alliances is their potential **to be a catalyst for delivering real innovation**. As noted in the

"What Is a Strategic Alliance?" section, at Florida Hospital strategic alliances are undertaken with a commitment to innovate. For example, in 1997 Florida Hospital worked with its allies to create a destination surgical training site at Celebration Health that is now known as the Nicholson Center for Surgical Advancement (NCSA). The purpose of NCSA is to raise the skills of healthcare providers around the world and dramatically enhance outcomes for patients in their own countries. In 2008, the NCSA trained over 6,000 physicians. In 2010, through key alliance relationships, the NCSA will be enhanced to enlarge the capacity with a new state-of-the-art training center designed to train more than 20,000 healthcare providers each year. That includes surgeons, surgical teams, and other allied health professionals. The NCSA includes a large, multi-specialty robotic surgery training program that is changing the way we may all undergo surgery in the future. This is one example of how Florida Hospital innovates to solve the challenges we all face in the coming healthcare reformation.

> For Florida Hospital and others in the healthcare industry, strategic alliances will be a tool used more frequently in the future to ensure the achievement of our mission. In fact, researchers concluded in a recent study on the frequency of alliances that "success [in the healthcare industry] will almost certainly require a greatly expanded use of alliances . . . in an increasingly dynamic healthcare ecosystem."[2]

WHY IS INNOVATION AT THE CORE?

AT FLORIDA HOSPITAL, WE UNDERSTAND that challenges in delivering healthcare today will be exponentially magnified in the future. Innovation is essential to meet these challenges, and without innovation we will fail—it is that simple.   As A. G. Lafley, chairman and CEO of Procter & Gamble, writes in his book, *The Game-Changer,* "My job at Procter & Gamble is focused on integrating innovation into *everything* we do. . . . Innovation must be the central driving force for any business that wants to grow and succeed in both the short and long terms."[3] This begs the question: so what is "innovation?" As I said earlier, definitions are crucial. Innovation at the most basic level must deliver strategic value to the enterprise. No longer is innovation something the R&D department handles alone.

While innovation still can include development of products and services in a traditional sense, most progressive companies have expanded their definition to include novel improvements to key business processes and new business model development as well as "open innovation" (looking to external sources). In fact, some studies have shown the greatest potential for innovation lies in areas not traditionally thought of as fertile ground, i.e., finance, business models, networking, core process, enabling process, and customer experience.

A full review of innovation is not possible within the scope of this monograph, but suffice it to say that innovation will continue to be a driving force enabling the achievement of our mission at Florida Hospital.   Our president, Lars Houmann, reminds us often that current business models in healthcare are not the tools that will sustain us and enable us to achieve our mission in the future.   As a part of our "retooling" to meet the needs of the future, we have determined that the continuation and further development of our "Strategic Innovation Agenda" (SIA) will provide the focus of our innovation energy.

Florida Hospital's *Strategic Innovation Agenda*
- **Elevate patient safety and clinical excellence**
- **"Excelerate" core process improvement**

- **Enrich our patients' experience**
- **Extend our care continuum**
- **Engage our community**

We believe innovation is the key to unlocking the future, and alliances are a key to unlocking innovation. We need to align with companies that have a similar commitment to innovate, as evidenced by their own version of the "innovation agenda" and deployment of it. To innovate, by any definition, requires attention, commitment, and resources on the part of any company and of everyone in it. The SIA will guide us in setting these priorities for our innovation. We have determined that all of our future alliance relationships should be grounded in the commitment to cooperatively innovate around the SIA to ensure internal alignment and adequate resources.

This innovation alignment allows us to leverage our core competencies and keeps us focused on our strategic imperatives. The compelling rewards to be gained from engaging in innovation through a disciplined process can be accelerated by collaboration with like-minded companies that recognize we can do more together than we can apart. Building and achieving a healthy "codependency" that, with the goal of innovation, drives us toward each other rather than apart is arguably the "holy grail" of alliance work.

TYPES OF ALLIANCES

A T FLORIDA HOSPITAL, WE CALL our strategic alliances **STARs**— **ST**rategic **A**lliance **R**elationships. Such relationships can be categorized as five types, represented in the figure below as points on the five-pointed star.

Our STAR Alliances may encompass one or several points on the star. They may encompass all five. Some may be heavily weighted to one type of alliance but still contain aspects of other types. Each alliance is unique in its goals and

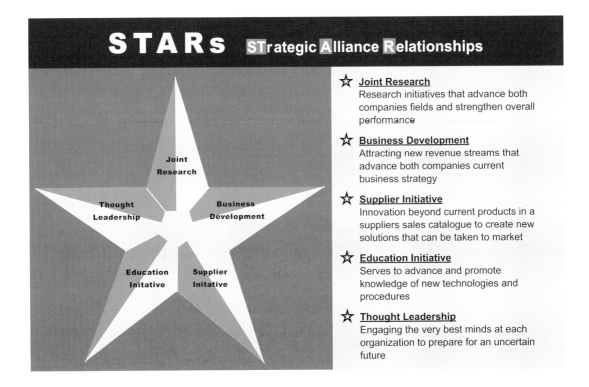

particulars, and each is undertaken because both parties agree the alliance can accomplish worthwhile objectives.

A **BUSINESS DEVELOPMENT** relationship charts a course for attracting new revenue streams that advance both companies' current business strategy. Many of our alliance relationships involve an element of business development that can range from alpha site product design and development to rapid acceleration of newly-introduced products to market. An example of both is Florida Hospital's advanced defibrillator development project with Philips Healthcare. Philips sought to design a new device that is a defibrillator, patient monitor, and twelve-lead EKG device. To translate this innovative idea into reality, Philips tapped into its longstanding alliance relationship with Florida Hospital, working with our clinical teams to confirm the overall strategy and product platform and tweak the human interface with the product. With this project, Florida Hospital participated in the launch of a product that reflected the specific needs of our clinicians, enhancing patient safety and outcomes.

Recognizing the value of such projects, Florida Hospital has built opportunities for business development collaboration into its short- and long-term plans. For example, we intend to develop more venues where industry can effectively collaborate with physicians, clinical staff, and hospital administrators to innovate the next generation of healthcare delivery in the operating room. The vision is to collaboratively test new products, processes, techniques, and business models that will drive superior patient outcomes.

A **RESEARCH** relationship enables both companies to undertake joint research initiatives to advance their fields and strengthen their performance. At Florida Hospital, we strive to use research results to improve patient outcomes. To this end, in 2009 we formed an alliance with the Burnham Institute for Medical Research to take the prevention, diagnosis, and treatment of diabetes and obesity to the next level. The Florida Hospital-Burnham Clinical Research Institute will study diabetes' effects on the heart and work to establish preventive treatments. It will essentially translate the world-class research of the Burnham Institute to the hospital bedside using the resources—including its large patient populations—of Florida Hospital, as well as the Cardiovascular Institute and Diabetes Institute. At the announcement of the Florida Hospital-Burnham Clinical Research Institute on August 17, 2009, Dr. Steven Smith, M.D., executive director of the new alliance, noted that "the new institute will help break down the distance that exists between research and the clinic."

Our goal on this point of the star is to create "collabortories," research collaborations between experts from different companies. Such heavy-hitters as IBM, Hewlett-Packard, Procter & Gamble, and Eli Lilly have recently adopted this strategic departure from the way corporations conducted research in the past. One commentator observed that the collabortory is a way companies can diversify their research portfolios, leverage what they already have, and obtain new knowledge and inventions.[4]

Speaking of a recent collaboration between IBM and a university in Saudi Arabia, the university's chief technology officer said it best: "[This] is a magnet for smart people, and makes it possible for us to solve big problems." This is the objective of Florida Hospital's research alliances—to bring together smart people to solve big problems, making history together.

A **SUPPLIER INITIATIVE** relationship, in the context of a strategic alliance, must have different goals than those of a potential purchase and sale transaction. It must undertake to innovate beyond the solutions that are already in the sales catalogue of a supplier.

We don't mean to underestimate the value of the supply chain relationship for both purchaser and seller—after all, many times that relationship is what brought the companies together in the first place. But in the move to the alliance relationship, the parties are now focused on creating solutions together that will impact the industry, not just Florida Hospital and the supplier. This is the "Blue Ocean" thinking I referred to earlier.

As Don Jernigan, then president and CEO of Florida Hospital, said in his address to the 2003 National Council of Presidents:

> The transactional relationship between suppliers and hospitals is inadequate to address the issues of the future. We need to redefine our relationship to align incentives that will allow us to succeed as we improve quality and reduce cost. Florida Hospital (and every company) must create new ways of working with vendors to address the care process as a whole as opposed to simply seeking to increase transactions. In fact, we need to reduce the inputs into the system if we are to achieve a sustainable future.

One example of an alliance that focused on innovating supplier solutions is one we formed early on with Agfa Corporation. Together we developed a new risk-sharing business model that enabled the installation of cutting-edge diagnostic imaging technology at Celebration Health and eventually throughout all Florida Hospital locations. Agfa, a longtime leader in radiographic film technology, developed software for PACS (Picture Archiving and Communication System). This technology digitizes radiologic images, such as CT scans, MRI, and ultrasound into high-resolution images that can be viewed on a monitor screen rather than printed on film. The system enables greatly improved image quality, in addition to efficiencies in transmission and storage. Doctors at multiple locations can simultaneously view the images for consultations, and during ongoing treatment can compare them with the patient's previous images stored digitally in the system and available with a few keystrokes.

Florida Hospital has found that the considerable upfront expense of PACS is greatly offset by time and cost savings, compared with the old system of printing, storing and transporting hard copies of the images. There is also the benefit to patients of faster and more accurate diagnoses. Agfa developed a new market strategy with Florida Hospital as the collaborator, giving it valuable insights into what hospitals would deem a compelling value proposition as it rolled out the product. Agfa was first to market with the new business model, which accelerated market growth for Agfa nationwide.

An **EDUCATION INITIATIVE** relationship serves to advance and promote knowledge of new technologies and procedures. An important part of Florida Hospital's mission is to keep its physicians and allied health professionals current in the latest advances and also to teach cutting-edge medicine to other healthcare providers. For example, Florida Hospital's leadership in minimally invasive surgery makes it a natural demonstration site for the latest techniques and instruments, and our strategic alliances advance that goal. In 2008, we established the Global Robotics Institute, a robotic surgery Center of Excellence at Florida Hospital, in an alliance with Intuitive Surgical. Intuitive is the maker of the da Vinci robot, which leads the way in the relatively new field of robotic laparoscopic surgery of the prostate, uterus, and kidney. Florida Hospital physicians have performed thousands of surgeries using da Vinci, and the Global Robotics Institute brings in other physicians from around the world to be trained by our experts. Those physicians return to their hospitals able to perform procedures using Intuitive Surgical's technology and techniques taught by Florida Hospital surgeons. And as a recognized market leader in robotic surgery, Florida Hospital attracts world-class surgical talent and receives referrals of patients from across the globe, further strengthening its brand and ability to extend its mission.

A **THOUGHT LEADERSHIP** relationship recognizes that we cannot solve the challenges of tomorrow alone. Through our alliances we have engaged the very best minds in healthcare to prepare for an uncertain future. A tangible expression of this is our biennial National Council of Presidents meeting, at which we convene the leaders of our alliance companies for the purpose of examining and testing Florida Hospital's assumptions and strategies. This forum requires a high level of transparency among all participants. Our alliance companies have told us that this is one of the most beneficial aspects of the alliance relationship with Florida Hospital, because it gives them unusual insight into the plans of an industry leader. Another way in which we drive thought leadership is in our steering committee meetings with various alliance companies throughout the year. At these forums, Florida Hospital and our allies share information that helps us chart where the healthcare industry is moving and become better able to plan for the future. This is perhaps one of the most significant benefits of the strategic alliance relationship.

EXPLORING A GOOD FIT BETWEEN ALLIES

BEFORE ALLIES JOIN FORCES and invest in a new relationship, it is essential for each to know who they are "saddling up with" and evaluate the "fit." The initial evaluation of a new alliance company should include such dimensions as leadership and vision, corporate culture, strategic direction, and capabilities and resources. The following questions can be used internally and as an outline for discussions with potential allies to evaluate the fit.

Alliance Company Selection Questions

1. Are they in a *Leadership Position* in their field?

2. Do they have a *Commitment to Innovate*?

3. Do we have *Shared Values*?

4. Is there a *Strategic Fit Between Our Key Goals*?

5. Can we *Support Each Other's Missions*?

6. Will they commit resources to *Advance the Vision*?

7. How do we *Make History Together*?

These are the types of questions that Florida Hospital's leadership team—led by Des Cummings, Jr., Ph.D., executive vice president—explored as they worked to build the strategic alliances that would make it possible to build the hospital of the future, Florida Hospital Celebration Health. And they continue to inform our thinking at Florida Hospital Strategic Venture Group as we explore possibilities for future alliances.

ENSURING ALIGNMENT

ONCE IT HAS BEEN ESTABLISHED that companies are a good fit, the next step in exploring a strategic alliance relationship is to carefully examine whether the proposed strategic alliance is indeed strategic to both parties. And, whether the premise of the alliance aligns with both parties' strategic intent. In other words, does this joint effort tie into both companies' strategic plans? Answering that question will determine the level of commitment and integration the relationship will enjoy. This is one of the most difficult aspects of alliance work to establish and maintain during the relationship.

Sometimes, what one or both parties believe is strategic is in reality a tactical initiative. Tactical initiatives are important but should not require the same structure, alignment, and resources as an alliance that is intended to be strategic. For example, suppose one of the hospital's current vendor companies has agreed that it would like to align resources to advance an educational initiative focused on developing new healthcare techniques in Third World countries. Such an effort is indeed strategic to Florida Hospital and very much in line with our mission and vision to become a global pacesetter in healthcare delivery. The vendor may declare its intent to further penetrate a market and accelerate products to market in Third World countries. But alignment will decline rapidly if alliance meetings of executives become focused on how to sell more products to Florida Hospital rather than remaining focused on Third World countries and the aligned objectives.

Even where there is initial declared strategic alignment, things can (and do) change. Sometimes companies change, priorities change, or people change. The alliance's success requires careful planning at the outset of an alliance to ensure alignment for the long-term by anticipating potential changes. And it requires regular, ongoing communication and joint efforts to spot, as early as possible, unanticipated changes that could affect the alliance.

Florida Hospital Strategic Venture Group has designed an Alignment Matrix that helps us evaluate the strategic value of alliances we are considering. This graphic tool allows us to see how the project can fit into our strategic objectives. The sample Alignment Matrix pictured on the following page explores the strategic value of a fictional alliance.

In this matrix, the five core areas of Florida Hospital's Strategic Innovation Agenda (SIA)—Patient Safety/Clinical Excellence, Core Process Improvement,

STRATEGIC ALIGNMENT MAP

SUPER STAR, INC	STAR Alliance Relationship				
Strategic Innovation Agenda	Supplier	Business Development	Research	Education	Thought Leadership
Evaluate Patient Safety/Clinical Excellence	Alpha/Beta – safety solutions			Global Distance Learning via Nicholson Center for Surgical Advancment	Strategic Planning for Health Care Reform
"Excelerate" Core Process Improvement					
Enrich our Patients' Experience	Single Port Access Surgury product dev		Lighting in Emergency Department		
Extend our Care Continuum		Home Healthcare model dev			
Engage our Community			Translational Research Institute – Burnham Inst	Diabetes Patient Education	

Patient Experience, Care Continuum, and Community—are represented in the vertical column, and the five types of STAR Alliances —Supplier, Business Development, Research, Education, and Thought Leadership—are represented in the horizontal column. Behind each of the projects identified in the matrix there should be an operational plan guiding the efforts of both parties. Ideally, both parties to the alliance will have a similar tool illustrating how the projects align internally. In Florida Hospital's viewpoint, ensuring that a proposed project clearly fits on this matrix is a critical early step in determining if the given project warrants the commitment required to achieve success in the alliance.

Performing the kind of in-depth evaluations of another company, a potential ally, that are outlined in this section and the previous one ("Exploring a Good Fit Between Allies") is never an easy process. But it will be an *impossible* task without first establishing a commitment to transparency and establishing trust.

THE IMPORTANCE OF TRUST

SUCCESSFUL ALLIANCE WORK IS LARGELY DEFINED by good relationships and good process. One without the other may provide *some* limited value, but getting them both right provides exponential value for both parties.

Florida Hospital, an Adventist Health System enterprise, is a mission-driven organization riding on a financially focused engine. "Mission and margin" are a reality here. This reality has, in turn, provided Florida Hospital some unique opportunities to extend the mission through sound financial stewardship.

FLORIDA HOSPITAL MISSION:
"To extend the healing ministry of Christ"

FLORIDA HOSPITAL VISION:
"To become a global pacesetter delivering preeminent, faith-based health care"

We also understand that our mission is in fact a relationship—a relationship to our community and to the people we serve, including patients, physicians, ***and the companies with which we form alliances***. The quality of these relationships is in many ways a measure of our ability to achieve the mission, and without these relationships, we cannot achieve our mission.

All good relationships are built on a foundation of trust; without it, they will fail and be costly. Consider the current healthcare model and its set of relationships. Physicians don't trust insurance companies and hospitals, insurance companies don't trust providers, providers don't trust insurance companies, providers don't trust government, and the patient has lost trust in most everyone.

Dr. David Shore, founding director of the Trust Initiative at Harvard School of Public Health and author of *The Trust Crisis in Healthcare*, points out that there are enormous costs to the healthcare system because payers, providers, and patients continue to view each other with suspicion. Shore says, "Just as trust is good medicine, it is also good business; high levels of trust both further an organization's mission and help build its margin. *Indeed, it may not be too much to say that the organization that owns trust owns its marketplace*" [emphasis added].[5]

I think Stephen Covey has expressed the value of trust particularly well:

COVEY *"SPEED OF TRUST"* FORMULA

Here's a simple formula that will enable you to take trust from an intangible and unquantifiable variable to an indispensable factor that is both tangible and quantifiable. The formula is based on the critical insight: Trust always affects two outcomes—speed and cost. . . It's that simple, that real, that predictable."[6]

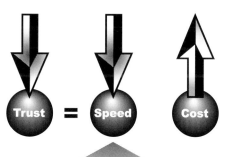

When trust goes down, speed will also go down and costs will go up.

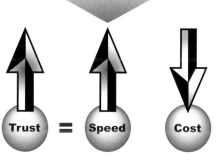

When trust goes up, speed will also go up and costs will go down.

Covey also refers to these other views on the economics of trust and speed:

"Our distrust is very expensive."
— RALPH WALDO EMERSON

"The world is changing very fast. Big will not beat small anymore. It will be the fast beating the slow."
— RUPERT MURDOCH, CHAIRMAN AND CEO, NEWS CORPORATION

"Mistrust doubles the cost of doing business."
— PROFESSOR JOHN WHITNEY, COLUMBIA BUSINESS SCHOOL [7]

Granted, various acceptable levels of success can be achieved between two or more parties without high levels of trust. For example, when a bank loans money for the purchase of a car, the transaction does not involve a high level of trust. The bank verifies statements of the borrower through credit checks and evaluates the person's ability to repay the loan. The loan has been collateralized to mitigate the risk of loss and, should the loan be paid in full, it equals success for the bank.

For an alliance to be as successful as it can be requires a level of trust between the companies that is not common and is difficult to achieve. This is one of the primary reasons alliances in general do not have a high success rate.[8]

BUILDING TRUST

IF THE BASIS OF A SUCCESSFUL ALLIANCE is a trusting relationship between allies, how do we go from the largely adversarial mindset of business-as-usual to a collaborative mindset of mutual trust? As one of my colleagues recently put it, how do we move from our positions *across* the negotiating table to *the same side* of the table? By building into the relationship what we'll call the **Three C's of Trust**:

- **COMMUNICATION:** From the outset of the relationship, senior executives and other key players must engage in candid dialogue and promote transparency so that each company's operations and goals are clearly detailed.

- **CHARACTER:** All dealings between the companies must be undertaken with a commitment to fairness and honesty that goes beyond that of the average business transaction. Both companies must have a track record of promises kept.

- **COMPETENCY:** Each company must commit to the project a team with the requisite skill sets to achieve all the alliance objectives. Skills and attributes needed in alliance team members include the following:

    o Credibility within their own organization.
    o Solid information network (internal and external).
    o Sound judgment.
    o Relationship-building skills.
    o Ability to handle ambiguity.

Developing trust in an alliance relationship is not easy, but here are a few "do's and don'ts" we have found that can build trust and make the relationship more collaborative and effective.

1. Don't get stuck in "selling" or "buying" mode, but do make the transition to collaboration mode.

2. Do foster transparency between the companies.

3. Do promote candid feedback.

4. Do align incentives with objectives (internally and externally).

5. Don't over-promise or under-deliver.

6. Do be interested in the alliance's success and in your allies' success—not just in your own company's success.

MANAGING THE ALLIANCE

A STRATEGIC ALLIANCE MUST HAVE A ROADMAP that promotes a clear understanding of objectives and the benefit to both organizations. It should be detailed but not overly so, using language that promotes flexibility as the project evolves. The goal is to be specific while avoiding tightly-worded "legalese" that constrains the parties to the point of stifling creativity and innovation.

The alliance's objectives should be clear; keep in mind that for the project to be worthwhile those objectives must also have a significant business impact with sustainable value. Objectives should also be achievable within the proposed duration of the alliance. Similarly, the project milestones, time-bound objectives, and metrics should be clearly detailed.

The management plan should also include the dedicated resource commitments of each company, including personnel resources. Florida Hospital decided early in the development of its alliance program to establish a dedicated alliance team that's now known as the Strategic Venture Group. This team is designed to learn from past alliances, establish best practices, and promote effective processes to create value in the alliance relationships. Additional resources from other business units are required to operationalize the alliance. In the case of Florida Hospital, that may include ownership from the clinical, finance, procurement, and management information systems (MIS) segments of our organization. Most of the time, our initiatives also require a physician champion to lead the way to adoption of new technologies and new surgical techniques.

A structure for joint decision-making and governance should be clearly established at the outset. Such a structure may include "ambassadors," or key point people in each company who are charged with representing the interests of the alliance company within their own company (see "The Role of Ambassadors" below). Other decision makers may include a steering committee, working groups, and additional support as needed.

Every alliance agreement should provide for regular "checkups:" high-level meetings to review progress and chart the future course. This is accomplished by the quarterly, semiannual, or annual steering committee meeting, at which executives and committee members evaluate past performance and establish new or revised operating plans for the future. In many cases, this forum leads to new initiatives that are strategic to both companies but were not contemplated at the outset of the relationship.

Maintaining strong relationships (between allied organizations and between individuals from those organizations who interact regularly to execute the alliance's work) is key to successful strategic alliance management. Even if the companies have established a virtually fail-proof process and procedures to achieve the alliance goals, if relations between the alliance companies sour, those processes and procedures can quickly break down. Conversely, a strong relationship can help the parties achieve results beyond those originally envisioned.

What can cause an alliance relationship to fail? Here are just some of the possible origins:

- One or both parties underestimate the investment of resources.
- Senior executive personal engagement is peripheral or absent.
- One or both parties underestimate the effort needed to collaborate effectively.

- The alliance is lacking clear objectives.
- One of the parties misrepresents their company's alignment with the objectives (i.e., lack of internal support).

Conversely, research conducted in 2006 has demonstrated, and our own experience has confirmed, that the following key corporate capabilities lead to the capture of alliance value and ensure alliance success:

1. **Building and maintaining internal alignment.** The development of a corporate vocabulary to define the components of the alliance strategy and its objectives is the first step to successful alignment of the alliance with the corporate strategy. If the team does not know or agree on the alliance strategy, attempting to capture value from the alliance will be a frustrating experience.

2. **Evaluating and considering relationship fit with potential partners.** Several criteria can be developed to evaluate the fit, and they should include as strategic goals the financial strength and compatibility of the mission and vision of both companies. The personality fit is also important and should not be minimized. The reality is that sometimes the personalities of key players just don't mesh. That may be workable for a transactional relationship, but to realize the maximum value from alliances, there must be a personality fit that works for both companies.

3. **Building strong working relationships while negotiating optimal deals.** The ability to build trust and maintain a strong relationship while negotiating is an art form. Both members of the alliance need to feel like they have a good deal. Tools can be developed to facilitate the negotiation process while building trust into the long term. One author from the alliance management consulting firm, Vantage Partners, put it simply—but profoundly: "Negotiate as if implementation

matters." [9]   After the signing of the agreement, both parties now must live with it and make it work, so negotiating for short term wins will not be the best strategy for long term viability of the relationship that will maximize the creation of strategic value.

4. **Establishing common ground rules for working together.** Decision making, communication, escalation of issues, and general governance issues should all be decided early on in the relationship. Everyone should know the ground rules and process for working together.

5. **Having dedicated alliance managers.** "Managers" here includes the many roles that touch the alliance, including the "ambassador" described in the next section and the day–to-day manager executing the alliance objectives. These managers must be committed to the success of the alliance but may not necessarily be devoted to the alliance full-time. In addition to their time, the commitment from all the managers should stem from a vision for the alliance that is passionate and focused.

6. **Having a collaborative corporate mindset.** Developing a culture that encourages collaborative behaviors throughout the enterprise is a key to alliance success. Moving to collaboration from an adversarial mindset is no small task. It will require training in collaborative behaviors as well as consistent encouragement and support from the top levels of the organization. Without a high level of collaborative skills throughout the corporation, alliance efforts will be marginalized and short lived.

7. **Managing multiple relationships with the same partner.** Most of the alliances companies at Florida Hospital have multiple relationships with us, including a supplier relationship. While the scope of the alliance may not include the supplier relationship, being able to manage these multiple relationships becomes very important, both from

a relationship and regulatory viewpoint. Because of the complex nature of the healthcare regulatory environment, it is imperative that all our Florida Hospital team and the alliance company team are aware of the multi-relational aspects of the alliance and adhere to the highest level of ethical conduct. Anything less will undermine credibility and trust and doom the alliance.

8. **Managing changes that affect alliances.** Companies engaged in alliances should develop a process by which each company regularly informs the other of changes to its strategy, structure, market, key personnel, and product offerings. Early exchange of this type information allows the alliance to prepare for and adjust to changes that impact its performance. [9]

THE ROLE OF AMBASSADORS

AS NOTED EARLIER, FOR EACH ALLIANCE, Florida Hospital appoints an "ambassador" who serves as its executive sponsor. Established best practices in alliance management generally recognize that the executive sponsor is a key component to achieving objectives and creating value in the alliance relationship. The ambassador is a senior-level executive who is capable of thinking holistically about the relationship, of being an advocate for the goals of the alliance, and of representing the alliance company in internal decisions affecting the alliance. The ambassador is essentially the "evangelist" for the alliance.

The ambassador plays an important role in helping the ally navigate the organization, particularly in a large, complex organization. A strong ambassador can initiate alliance discussions at the rights levels within the organization that will create additional opportunities for the alliance. The ambassador is not engaged in the day-to-day operations of the alliance work but rather serves in an executive function, monitoring the status of the relationship and the achievements of the alliance. Ideally, the ambassador is the key stakeholder in the alliance's performance and success. Thus, it is helpful to have alliance performance aligned with the ambassador's accountabilities. The ambassador must understand the value of the alliance, not just to his or her own areas of responsibility but to the entire enterprise.

THE LIFE CYCLE OF THE ALLIANCE

EVEN WITH THE BEST INTENTIONS, many of the alliances that are formed fail to achieve their stated goals. Even those that can be declared a success will have a natural life cycle. In this fast-changing world, the drivers that bring the parties together initially can alter dramatically over a short time period. Therefore, from the outset of the relationship, all parties to the alliance must plan for a graceful termination.

At Florida Hospital, we've found that most alliance relationships will have a five-year initial term. But the end to an initial term for the alliance does not necessarily mean the end to the relationship. Frequently, the allies will find that they want to continue working together on existing projects and expand the relationship to new ventures. At that point, they continue the creative process of envisioning fresh areas for innovation.

THE JOURNEY CONTINUES

IN THE YEARS SINCE FLORIDA HOSPITAL BEGAN exploring the power of strategic alliances, back when we were planning Celebration Health, we have learned a number of valuable lessons.

Chief among those lessons is that, at the end of the day, it's all about relationships. Strategic alliances are hard work; they are complex and sometimes not as clear-cut as we might like. It is out of these challenges that significant value can be created for the members of the alliance, and a strong relationship serves as the rails that will keep it on track. A strategic alliance relationship is not like a merger or acquisition. With the latter, one company can simply mandate the actions of another and the identity of one is subject to the identity of another. On the other end of the spectrum of corporate relationships, a strategic alliance cannot be covered in a simple, single contract for the provision of goods and services; true alliances are more fluid and dynamic than what can be contained or contemplated in the four corners of a contract. Alliance relationships rise and fall on a mutual desire and commitment to collaborate. But collaboration is a learned behavior, and some companies learn better than others.

Florida Hospital has also found that alliance relationships focused on innovation and built on a commitment to building trust can enable allies to leverage one another's core competencies and create sustainable value. That value can be measured by expanding markets, providing a competitive advantage and/or growth of a company. For those companies that can achieve a sustainable capability to cooperate, the return on investment should be exponential, allowing those companies to achieve their respective missions in ways that they could not accomplish alone and, indeed, make history together.

APPENDIX
FLORIDA HOSPITAL ALLIANCE COMPANIES

THIS LIST INCLUDES ALL OF THE COMPANIES with which Florida Hospital has formed alliances, past and present, since the inception of our strategic alliance initiatives (in alphabetical order):

FLORIDA HOSPITAL ALLIANCE COMPANIES

Agfa Corporation	Hill-Rom Company, Inc.
Amgen Inc.	IBM
Bayer Corporation	IKON Office Solutions, Inc.
Bellsouth Corporation	Johnson & Johnson, Inc.
Boston Scientific Corporation	Mallinckrodt Inc.
Bristol-Myers Squibb Company	Medtronic, Inc.
Burnham Institute	Nike, Inc.
Buxton Company	Olympus Corp.
Cardinal Health	Philips Medical Systems
Cerner Corporation	Roche Diagnostics Corporation
Cordis Corporation	Steris Corporation
Crothall Facilities Management Inc.	Karl Storz Endoscopy-America, Inc.
DeRoyal Industries, Inc.	Stryker, Inc.
Ethicon Inc.	Varian, Inc.
Ethicon Endo-Surgery, Inc.	Walt Disney World Co.
GE Healthcare Inc.	

NOTES

1. W. Chan Kim and Renée Mauborgne, *Blue Ocean Strategy* (Boston: Harvard Business School Press, 2005), 3–5.

2. Jonathan Hughes and Laura Visioni, *Alliances in the Healthcare Industry: Report of Study Findings.* (Boston: Vantage Partners, 2009).

3. A. G. Lafley and Ram Charan, *The Game-Changer; How You Can Drive Revenue and Profit Growth with Innovation.* (New York: Crown Business, 2008), 1.

4. Steve Hamm, "Big Blue's Global Lab: How Big Blue is Forging Cutting-Edge Partnerships around the World," *Business Week* (August 27, 2009).

5. David A. Shore, "The (Sorry) State of Trust in the American Healthcare Enterprise," in *The Trust Crisis in Healthcare* (New York: Oxford University Press, 2007), 149.

6. Stephen M. R. Covey and Rebecca R. Merrill, *The Speed of Trust* (New York: Free Press, 2006), 13.

7. Ibid.

8. Danny Ertel, "Getting Past Yes," *Harvard Business Review* (November 1, 2004).

9. These principles are outlined in *Managing Alliances for Business Results: Lessons Learned from Leading Companies* (Boston: Vantage Partners, 2006) by Jeff Weiss, Sara Keen, and Stuart Kliman.

We would like to hear from you.
Please send your comments about this monograph
to us in care of Comments@FLHosp.org. Thank you.

ACKNOWLEDGEMENTS

MY SINCERE THANKS AND APPRECIATION goes to everyone who had a hand in making this publication a reality. I am especially grateful for the opportunity to prepare this monograph and to share a portion of what we at Florida Hospital have learned since the launch of Strategic Alliances at Celebration Health.

I am indebted to those who have gone before me to build the strategic alliance capability at Florida Hospital. Our organization is led by an extraordinary executive team. They are the ones who really developed the content for this monograph through their vision, hard work and determination. Lars Houmann, Brian Paradis, Des Cummings, and Eddie Soler not only helped create Strategic Alliances at Florida Hospital, they continue to support our work from the highest levels of the company. Des Cummings requires a special note of appreciation. His energy, creativity, and extraordinary vision inspire me and all who know him.

My appreciation also goes to Susan Mitchell and Jan Moysey in our Florida Hospital Strategic Venture Group for their professionalism and dedication to alliance work. Their superior skills and talents make our team uniquely suited for the alliance work we do each day at Florida Hospital.

I also want to thank the Florida Hospital Publishing team, including Todd Chobotar, Stephanie Rick, and Lillian Boyd. They provided the structure, coordination of resources, and encouragement that took this project across the finish line.

Most significantly, I want to thank my wife, Cindy, the love of my life. She and our children, Erica and Evan, are my most cherished blessings.

ABOUT THE AUTHOR

KEITH LOWE currently serves as Executive Director of the Strategic Venture Group at Florida Hospital where he manages the Strategic Alliance program. In this capacity he has overseen alliance relationships with some of the largest and most respected companies in America including Disney, Nike, GE, Johnson & Johnson, Philips, AGFA, and Stryker. As an attorney with over 22 years of experience, Keith has represented individual and business interests in a wide variety of both legal and business concerns.

Keith is a graduate of the Samford University, Cumberland School of Law where he received both his JD and MBA. In addition to his corporate experience, Keith has also served as an adjunct faculty member at several Florida colleges where he taught managerial finance, real property law and paralegal studies. With his combination of teaching and applied business experience Keith has become a sought-after speaker on topics such as Industry Growth through Innovation, Corporate Legal and Compliance Issues, and Strategic Alliances. He is also an ordained minister. Keith and his wife, Cindy, live in Orlando and have two adult children.

For information about Keith's speaking engagements, consulting, booking him as a speaker, or media interviews, please visit: www.FloridaHospitalPublishing.com.

FLORIDA HOSPITAL

The skill to heal. The spirit to care.

Florida Hospital Celebration Health

Florida Hospital Altamonte

GINSBURG

Florida Hospital Winter Park

Florida Hospital Orlando

Florida Hospital East Orlando

Florida Hospital Apopka

Florida Hospital Kissimmee

ABOUT FLORIDA HOSPITAL

For over one hundred years the mission of Florida Hospital has been: *To extend the health and healing ministry of Christ.* Opened in 1908, Florida Hospital is comprised of seven hospital campuses housing over 2,000 beds and eighteen walk-in medical centers. With over 16,000 employees—including 2,000 doctors and 4,000 nurses—Florida Hospital serves the residents and guests of Orlando, the No. 1 tourist destination in the world. Florida Hospital cares for over one million patients a year. Florida Hospital is a Christian, faith-based hospital that believes in providing Whole Person Care to all patients – mind, body and spirit.   Hospital fast facts include:

- **LARGEST ADMITTING HOSPITAL IN AMERICA.** Ranked No. 1 in the nation for inpatient admissions by the *American Hospital Association.*

- **AMERICA'S HEART HOSPITAL.** Ranked No. 1 in the nation for number of heart procedures performed each year, averaging 15,000 cases annually. MSNBC named Florida Hospital "America's Heart Hospital" for being the No. 1 hospital fighting America's No. 1 killer—heart disease.

- **HOSPITAL OF THE FUTURE.** At the turn of the century, the *Wall Street Journal* named Florida Hospital the "Hospital of the Future".

- **ONE OF AMERICA'S BEST HOSPITALS.** Recognized by *U.S. News & World Report* as "One of America's Best Hospitals" for ten years. Clinical specialties recognized have included: Cardiology, Orthopaedics, Neurology & Neurosurgery, Urology, Gynecology, Digestive Disorders, Hormonal Disorders, Kidney Disease, Ear, Nose & Throat and Endocrinology.

- **LEADER IN SENIOR CARE.** Florida Hospital serves the largest number of seniors in America through Medicare with a goal for each patient to experience a "Century of Health" by living to a healthy hundred.

- **TOP BIRTHING CENTER.** *Fit Pregnancy* magazine named Florida Hospital one of the "Top 10 Best Places in the Country to have a Baby". As a result, *The Discovery Health Channel* struck a three-year production deal with Florida Hospital to host a live broadcast called "Birth Day Live". Florida Hospital annually delivers over 9,000 babies.

- **CORPORATE ALLIANCES.** Florida Hospital maintains corporate alliance relationships with a select group of Fortune 500 companies including Disney, Nike, Johnson & Johnson, Philips, AGFA, and Stryker.

- **DISNEY PARTNERSHIP.** Florida Hospital is the Central Florida health & wellness resource of the *Walt Disney World* ® Resort. Florida Hospital also partnered with Disney to build the ground breaking health and wellness facility called Florida Hospital Celebration Health located in Disney's town of Celebration, Florida. Disney and Florida Hospital recently partnered to build a new state-of-the-art Children's Hospital.

- **HOSPITAL OF THE 21ST CENTURY.** Florida Hospital Celebration Health was awarded the *Premier Patient Services Innovator Award* as "The Model for Healthcare Delivery in the 21st Century".

- **SPORTS EXPERTS.** Florida Hospital is the official hospital of the Orlando *Magic* NBA basketball team. In addition, Florida Hospital has an enduring track record of providing exclusive medical care to many sports organizations. These organizations have included: Disney's Wide World of Sports, Walt Disney World's Marathon Weekend, the Capital One Bowl, and University of Central Florida Athletics. Florida Hospital has also provided comprehensive healthcare services for the World Cup and Olympics.

- **PRINT RECOGNITION.** Self magazine named Florida Hospital one of America's "Top 10 Hospitals for Women". *Modern Healthcare* magazine proclaimed it one of America's best hospitals for cardiac care.

- **CONSUMER CHOICE AWARD WINNER.** Florida Hospital has received the Consumer Choice Award from the *National Research Corporation* every year from 1996 to the present.

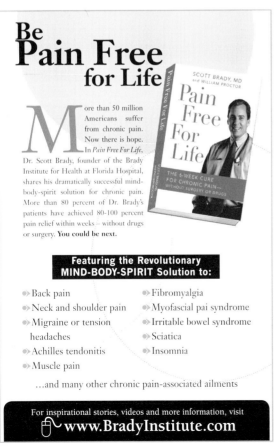